FOR MARIT ERIKSSON

Researched on location in Egypt and London.
Historical consultant: Dr Bill Manley, Subject Specialist in Archaeology
at the University of Glasgow and Research Associate
of the National Museums of Scotland.

Find out more about this book at www.mickandbrita.com

No living creatures were harmed during the making of this book.

Fly on the Wall: Pharaoh's Egypt copyright © Frances Lincoln Limited 2005
Text and illustrations copyright © Mick Manning and Brita Granström 2005

First published in Great Britain in 2005 by
Frances Lincoln Children's Books, 4 Torriano Mews,
Torriano Avenue, London NW5 2RZ

www.franceslincoln.com

Distributed in the USA by Publishers Group West

British Library Cataloguing in Publication Data available on request

ISBN 1-84507-100-X

Printed in Singapore

1 3 5 7 9 8 6 4 2

PHARAOH'S EGYPT

MICK MANNING & BRITA GRANSTRÖM

CONTENTS

FRANCES LINCOLN
CHILDREN'S BOOKS

WHO WERE THE ANCIENT EGYPTIANS?

The Pharaohs ruled Egypt from about 3000 BC to about 30 BC. Egyptians were clever and inventive. They used tools made of bronze and stone to do whatever they wanted. Ancient Egypt was a wonderful place, attracting people from many lands to visit and to buy and trade goods. Many of these visitors stayed and settled there, marrying Egyptians and worshipping the Egyptian gods. This story takes place around 1249 BC during the reign of a very famous Pharaoh, Ramesses II, also called Ramesses the Great, and in one of the most exciting periods of Ancient Egypt's history called the New Kingdom.

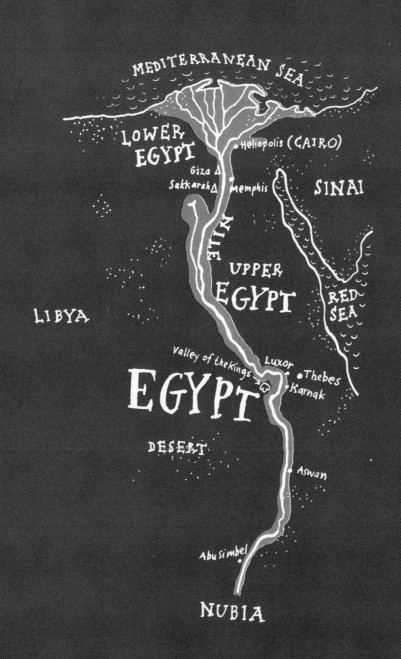

MEDITERRANEAN SEA

LOWER EGYPT

Heliopolis (CAIRO)

Giza △

Sakkarah △ Memphis

SINAI

NILE

UPPER EGYPT

RED SEA

LIBYA

Valley of the Kings Luxor

EGYPT

Thebes

Karnak

DESERT

Aswan

Abu Simbel

NUBIA

PHARAOH'S KINGDOM

Ramesses II's Egypt is a civilised country and he is a powerful king. Many different people live and have to work hard in the Pharaoh's New Kingdom. Let's look in on some of them as they go about their daily lives.

RAMESSES II
our Pharaoh

NEFERTARI
Queen of Egypt

SHABAKA
the High Priest

ASRU
a priestess

HUYA
an important scribe

DEDI and KIYA
Huya and Maya's
twin daughters

MAYA
Huya's wife

DAGI
a policeman

SEMTI
an embalmer
and Huya's
brother.

SUNRISE

This humming chariot, this blur of legs and wheels, is being raced by the Pharaoh himself! His people believe he is a god, powerful enough to make the sun rise and the river flood. This is Ramesses the Great!

Ramesses loves to race his chariot across the desert.

The royal chariot thunders along!

'Woof Woof!'

The word Pharaoh began as a nickname for the Egyptian king. It means 'great house' because everyone believed the king's human body was home to a god.

The Egyptians believed that Ra, the great sun god, drove his fiery chariot across the sky every day. They even nicknamed themselves 'Ra's Cattle'.

The pharaoh owns the best horses in Egypt.!

These pyramids are the tombs of Ancient Egyptian Pharaohs.

Fast hunting dogs known as 'pharaoh hounds'

The Egyptians call themselves 'Blacklanders' after the rich, fertile soil of the Nile valley.

By the time Ramesses II was on the throne, the Pharaohs had not used pyramids as tombs for hundreds of years.

The Great Pyramid at Giza had vents pointing to the constellation of Orion so the mummy's spirit could fly straight up to the gods.

SCRIBE

Huya woke up early to the sound of barking baboons. He is a scribe – a very important person in Pharaoh's Egypt. First he must wash, dress and eat breakfast, then a busy day lies ahead. Let's follow him and see where he takes us!

Shesh the house slave helps Maya get dressed.

A comfy bed made of leather straps on a wooden frame.

stool

head rests

Huya

magic stick to keep scorpions away

Scribes are VERY important people because they can read and write.

Shesh offers Huya's daughters some breakfast.

Dedi Kiya

Scribes could be clerks, secretaries and tax inspectors. Egyptians kept records of everything.

Ordinary people couldn't read or write. Those who could, were believed to have power from the gods!

10

Maya's garden is beautiful. It has flowers, fruit trees and even an ornamental pond with fish.

Grrrr!

this is Huya's writing equipment.

ink

pens

Baboons make good guards. They can be trained to pick dates too!

This statue of **THOTH**, the god of writing, is a gift from the Pharaoh!

cool air vent

Even Huya's town house is a reward from the Pharaoh!

The Ancient Egyptians believed that the god Thoth invented writing and passed its secret to humans. His symbols were a bird called an ibis and a baboon.

Baboons often sat and soaked up the first rays of the morning sun. The Egyptians thought it looked as if they were worshipping Ra!

CITY SIGHTS

Even a royal scribe walks his children to class sometimes.
The town is already busy: a papyrus workshop, a potter,
a goldsmith and a bead-maker. Sandal-makers work
here too – just down the alley!

Mats hung out to air

mudbrick houses

The streets smell of animal dung. a rich aroma!

It's noisy this morning! Miaow!"

Hee-haw!

Oink! Oink!

Living conditions for the poor could be bad, but many people lived well in mudbrick houses with windows and rooftop terraces.

Egyptian gold came from Kush, a province in southern Egypt. Prisoners were often sent to work in the gold mines.

Bead-makers can drill three beads at a time.

The drill **purrs** like a cat.

Threading beads

Beautiful jewellery!

stalks from the papyrus plant can be made into a lovely surface to write on.

Khnum, the ram-headed god of potters

soak, slice thinly, criss-cross, pound, smooth and let it dry.

slices of papyrus stalk

Pepi's pottery is always in demand!

Egyptians believed they were made from clay by the river god Khnum, on a potter's wheel.

Different types of food traded at the markets included peas, cucumbers, onions, garlic, flour, goats, chickens, ducks and eggs.

Homework - the boys have been practicing with pen and ink.

EAGLE

ARM

TWO STROKES

VIPER

FOOT

BASKET

HAND

COBRA

JAR

HOUSE

FLAX

LION

OWL

BAR

CROWN

LASSO

DOOR

SLOPE

POOL

LOAF

ROPE

DOUBLE REED

BOLT

Huya and the girls

The writing school is also in the temple.

Hieroglyphs were a way of writing with pictures. Some pictures could mean individual letters, others meant whole words.

The Egyptians also wrote on bits of stone and broken pottery called ostraca.

14

AT THE TEMPLE

The temple is huge and breathtaking! Boys from important families learn reading and writing here. Girls like Dedi and Kiya are taught temple dances. Huya teaches them to read and write at home.

Dedi and Kiya love to dance

"Be a scribe. He is the controller of everyone!"

Boys study reading, writing and arithmetic at the temple school.

clay slate

ink palette

water

water clock

Children's toys included dolls made of painted wood, toy animals and marbles.

Water-clocks worked by measuring water as it slowly dripped away. As the level in the bucket dropped, marks on the side showed the time.

PRIESTS AND GODS

Huya's first appointment is with the High Priest. Huya is listing the offerings people have brought to the temple and left for the gods. People brought bread, meat and animal mummies yesterday. Today it's still very early, but one cat mummy has arrived already!

The temple is huge and cool inside!

Cats are the symbol of Bastet, a fertility goddess.

Food offerings such as bread, meat and wine were shared out among the priests – they lived well!

Priests didn't hold services like the ones in today's churches or temples. Their job was to look after the gods, making sure they didn't abandon Egypt.

In the inner sanctum a priest is singing to wake up **Ra**, lord of the gods.

Smoky clouds of incense smell delicious - so does **Asru** the priestess!

This priest is called the 'Keeper of the crocodile'!

Lovely fresh flowers from the temple's gardener

Watch Out! The sacred crocodile is escaping again! He is a symbol of **Sobek**, a crocodile-headed water god...

Bes are comic dwarf gods who bring good luck.

Egyptians believed in a natural balance between good and bad, order and chaos. This was called 'maat'.

Every big city supported one favourite god – a bit like people who support football teams today!

THE NILE

Huya's next visit takes him upriver. Huya loves the Nile. Without its seasonal flood of rich river mud, the black soil would dry up and the red desert sand would take over. Then the Blacklanders would starve!

The ship with its sail up is going south.

This man steers the boat.

Huya

This boat is made of wood.

splish! splash! splosh!

Desert-red was the Egyptian colour of death while soil-black was the colour of life.

Khnum, the ram-headed god, also controlled the seasonal flooding of the Nile, which could mean a good harvest or starvation.

Most goods are transported by river. Ships with their sails down are travelling north.

Lotus flowers symbolise Upper Egypt and rebirth.

Small boats made of woven papyrus are a common sight.

This man checks the depth with a long pole.

The Nile is teeming with wildlife...

An ibis and an egret, two water birds of the Nile.

papyrus

The Egyptians needed to know when the Nile would flood and this led to the development of the world's first calendar.

Boatbuilders were highly valued as timber was rare and expensive. Bundles of reeds were used to make everyday boats.

FARMING

This year Khnum gave the Blacklanders a perfect flood. The crops have grown well and now they must be harvested. It's a busy time for the farmers. Grain must be threshed and the flax must be cut. The harvest must be gathered in safely and recorded by scribes like Huya.

Grain is stored in mudbrick granaries.

It's not as easy as it looks!

Farm animals are counted too.

palm trees grow sweet dates.

Quack! Quack! Honk!

Sometimes there were plagues of locusts that ate all the crops. This could mean starvation for the Egyptians.

After the harvest, peasants were often forced to do road repairs, build temples or serve in the army.

Not many locusts this year.

Harvesting the crop. The wooden sickles have flint blades.

"Go away, demons of Seth!"

Huya counts the harvest. "One, TWO..."

Part of the harvest is taken for the Pharaoh and his temples.

Egyptian farmers grow barley and a sort of wheat for food, and flax to make linen clothes.

Legend tells us that the god Osiris taught the people how to farm. His wife, Isis, taught them how to make beer and bread.

The story of Osiris being reborn from the underworld was a myth explaining the planting and harvesting of barley.

Some statues were carved on the spot, others were hauled into place by work gangs who competed with each other to be the best.

Sculptors and master craftsmen were valued as highly as priests. Some even had their own tombs built!

HEAVE-HO!

A great temple is taking shape! Hundreds of stones have already been dragged into place. Day after day, year after year, hand over sweaty hand, inch by back-breaking inch.

It's baking HOT!

The gang is about to take a breather...

Workers worked for eight days. Then they had two days of rest. The temples at Karnak took a thousand years to build.

The tomb builders had their own guarded villages. They were well fed and looked after because their work was so important.

THE QUEEN'S TOMB

Further upriver, Huya checks on the supplies sent to the tomb builders. This will be Nefertari's tomb one day. Huya hopes his queen will live for a long time yet, but he thinks this is the greatest tomb he has ever seen!

Royal tombs can take a lifetime to build. Sometimes they are started before the owner is born!

This artist is painting Anubis, god of the dead, on a tomb wall.

Anubis protected the mummy from evil spirits. His symbol was the jackal, a desert animal often heard howling around burial grounds at night.

Healed broken limbs and even amputations found on skeletons show that the Egyptians were clever doctors.

Rich people could afford lavish tombs which they could spend the rest of their lives decorating and redecorating.

Many people, rich and poor, died young because of damp housing, stomach illnesses, breathing problems and parasites.

THE MUMMY-MAKERS

The embalmer's workshop is nicknamed the 'house of perfection' but it stinks in here! Visiting the mummy-makers always spoils Huya's lunch. Stand back — he's going to be sick!

the **Anubis** priest says magic words as the mummy is wrapped in bandages.

scarab beetle

Magic amulets are placed among the bandages to protect the mummy.

Anubis priest

these organs are saved in **canopic jars.**

STOMACH   LIVER   LUNGS   INTESTINES

clean linen wrapping

Natron is a sort of salt that dried out the body and helped preserve it.

Legend tells that Osiris was murdered by Seth but Isis wrapped him in bandages and he came back to life as a god of the dead – the first mummy!

Mud was pushed under the mummy's skin to pad it out. False eyes could be made from onions!

Only the rich could afford to be mummified properly. The poor only got a quick and cheap version.

How do you dress a Pharaoh?

It takes hours to dress Ramesses.

The double crown of Upper and Lower Egypt.

The crook and flail are symbols of power.

The cobra goddess is a symbol of kingship.

Wings of Horus protect the Pharaoh.

linen kilt

Nefertari wears the golden headdress of a vulture goddess.

PALACE LIFE

Back at the palace, life couldn't be more delicious!
The Pharaoh has invited many guests. While the music plays
and the dancers sway, the governors who rule his towns
and the generals of his army have to tell him what is going on
in his kingdom.

The rich wore the best quality linen.
The poor wore rougher linen or wool.

The oldest dress in the world came from Egypt.
It is 5000 years old!

The palace is full of ambitious nobles who will marry, or even kill, for power!

slaves with fans keep the royal couple cool.

dancing girls

LOVE POTION
Mix dandruff with barley wine and the blood of a tick from a black dog!

musicians

Perfumed cones of fat melt slowly on the head and scent the room!

nice-smelling Lotus flowers

fresh fruit and meat

honeycomb

Wigs are worn over shaved heads.

Women and men wear eye make-up.

Egyptians made sweets using dates, spices, nuts and honey mixed into a paste, then moulded into balls and dipped in ground almonds.

Chips of grindstone and blowing sand got into the flour, quickly wearing down people's teeth.

FUNERAL

People gather to watch as a coffin is hauled to its tomb on a boat-shaped sledge. The Pharaoh's police mingle with the crowd. They are hunting for a gang of tomb robbers and wonder if Huya has seen anything suspicious.

Relatives bring furniture and gifts for the tomb.

"Waahhh! Waahhh!"

Mourners are paid to sob and throw ashes and flower petals to make the dead look important.

sarcophagus

Small wooden models of people are put in the tomb – to be servants in the next life!

Egyptians believe the gods judge and decide if the dead shall enter the Egyptian afterlife.

This painting shows the 'weighing of the heart' ceremony in the afterlife.

The 'opening of the mouth' ceremony sets the spirit free.

Oxen pull the sledge.

An Anubis priest leads the procession.

Anubis weighs the dead person's heart against 'the feather of balance.' Osiris judges while Thoth writes down the result.

If the dead person's heart is heavy with bad deeds it is eaten by a fierce monster.

Inside the air is very stale!

TOMB ROBBERS

The night is full of shadows. Has Seth sent his demons to haunt the Blacklanders? No! Tomb robbers have broken into a tomb: ripping and unwrapping, stealing from the dead.

Valuable brooches and jewels are tucked in amongst the bandages!

Many Pharaohs were buried in a rocky place in the desert called the Valley of the Kings.

Wealthy Egyptians took many possessions with them for use in the afterlife. Rich pickings for robbers – and archaeologists!

smoky torchlight.

Dark and spooky!

Precious things are placed with the dead for their journey to the after life.

Girdle of Isis and Eye of Horus are protective amulets against evil.

A make-up box showing the sky goddess, Nut

A solid gold goddess!

Fish amulet protects people from drowning.

hall of chariots

entrance corridor

shaft!

burial chamber

hidden stairs!

A vulture goddess of Upper Egypt

Tomb robbers often had inside help from palace officials who wanted a share of the riches.

Secret tombs were cut deep into the rock – but some were still found and robbed.

Ramesses watches the stars waiting for a sign... Faraway, a jackal howls in the dark.!

Egyptians knew Jupiter, Mars, Mercury, Saturn and Venus. They had names for them like 'god of the morning' or 'bull of the sky'.

Tomb paintings show star constellations and planets as gods sailing the sky in boats. They were known as the 'stars that know no rest'.

STARGAZERS

This starry night Ramesses is thanking the gods for the harvest. Did they just hear a message from Anubis? The Pharaoh and his priests gaze up in wonder at the 'stars that know no rest' and feel sure he was telling them that their Blackland is blessed.

Sirius and Orion represented star gods that marked seasonal changes for the Ancient Egyptians.

The Pharaoh and his priests performed many rituals through the year to ask favours from, or give thanks to, the gods.

END OF THE PHARAOHS

The New Kingdom came to an end following the death of Ramesses XI. By 525 BC Egypt had become part of the Persian Empire and although Egyptian rulers had regained Egypt's independence in wars by 332 BC, the Egyptian kingdom was passed to the Greeks. The last Pharaoh born in Egypt was the famous Cleopatra VII. Finally in 30 BC Egypt was invaded and conquered by the Romans. The Roman emperors ruled Egypt as Pharaohs and some, such as Hadrian (the same emperor that built Hadrian's Wall on the northern frontier of Britain), took their duties as Pharaoh very seriously.

WHAT THE PHARAOHS LEFT BEHIND . . .

The Ancient Egyptians made many discoveries in medicine, surgery and farming. They were expert surveyors and quarrymen. They were also among the earliest to use town planning, taxation and a police force. But they are remembered most for their amazing statues, temples and pyramids. Egyptian hieroglyphics (their clever picture writing) was decoded in the 1800s and now experts can learn much about their lives by reading the inscriptions on tomb walls and on tablets and papyrus recorded by people like Huya, the scribe. Legends and tales of mystery continue to be made up about the gods of Ancient Egypt. Scary stories about mummies coming to life have been told for centuries. Exciting films and computer games continue the story today.

AFTERLIFE – pages 30, 31, 32 & 33.
The Ancient Egyptian 'heaven' where there would be fields of plenty and massive harvests.
ANUBIS – pages 24, 26, 31 & 35.
A god of the dead, embalming and mummification.
CANOPIC JARS – page 26.
Special jars used to store the mummy's lungs, liver, stomach and intestines.
CONSTELLATIONS – pages 9 & 34.
Star patterns in the sky.
EMBALMERS – pages 7, 26 & 27.
The skilled workers who prepared the mummies.
GOLDSMITHS – page 12.
Craftsmen who made golden jewellery and precious objects. Most gold came from Kush, a province in southern Egypt.
HIEROGLYPHS – page 14.
The picture writing of the Ancient Egyptians.
HORUS – pages 25, 28 & 33.
A hawk–headed god, son of Osiris and Isis and defender of good against the evil of Seth.
INCENSE – page 16.
A perfume that is burned slowly and makes nice, smelly smoke.
ISIS – pages 21, 25 & 26.
A fertility goddess and 'mother of Egypt'. She was the wife of Osiris.
JACKAL – pages 24, 34 & 35.
A small wild dog that lives in the desert. Commonly seen around burial grounds, it was the symbol of Anubis, protector god of the dead.
KUSH – page 12.
A southern province in Egypt. For many years, Kush was ruled by the Pharaohs. Long after Ramesses II, during the 25th Dynasty, the Kushites ruled Egypt as Pharaohs and left behind many fine buildings.
KHNUM – pages 13, 18 & 20.
The ram–headed god that controlled the important flooding of the Nile. He created humans on a heavenly potter's wheel so was also the god of potters.
MUDBRICK HOUSES – pages 12 & 20.
Buildings made from mud and straw.

GLOSSARY & INDEX